A true story from the Bible

Bartimaeus was sad.

He could not see. His eyes did not work.

But he could hear.

Stomp, stamp, clomp, tramp!

Lots of feet.

And lots of voices.

Jesus was coming!

Jesus!?

Bartimaeus opened his mouth
as big and wide as he could and shouted,

VERY

LOUDLY

Jesus!
The best

"Shhhhhh"

"Be quiet!"

"Too loud!"

    "Not you!"

everyone said.

But Bartimaeus
was not quiet!

He opened his mouth
even wider

and shouted

EVEN

LOUDER.

And – stomp, stamp, clomp ... stop!
Jesus stopped ...
and called Bartimaeus!

"You're all better!" Jesus said,
    "You believed in me, so now you can see."

    And suddenly Bartimaeus could see!

Bartimaeus saw something
no one else could see ...

The King GOD said was coming

... had come!

The King God sent to make things better
... and not just eyes.

And that was someone
worth shouting about!

Notes for grown-ups

This story comes from Mark 10 v 46-52. Bartimaeus was a blind beggar, but he could see who Jesus really was. He called Jesus the "Son of David", another name for the *Christ*, God's promised perfect King, who would be from the family of King David.

So in this story we call Jesus *"the best King EVER! The one God said was coming!"* Bartimaeus believed that Jesus was the promised King, and also that Jesus could heal him.

"I want to see," he told Jesus. *"Go,"* said Jesus, *"your faith has healed you." Immediately he received his sight and followed Jesus along the road* (v 51-52, NIV). Bartimaeus believed in Jesus and followed him. Jesus welcomes everyone who believes in him and wants to follow him.

In the story, we also call Jesus *"the King God sent to make things better... and not just eyes"*. The Bible tells us that we are separated from God by our sin—the wrong things we do, say and think. Jesus came to make this better. If we trust in Jesus, we can have our sin forgiven and be friends with God for ever.

Mark 10 v 46-52

(The Bible: New International Version)

[46] Then they came to Jericho. As Jesus and his disciples, together with a large crowd, were leaving the city, a blind man, Bartimaeus (which means "son of Timaeus"), was sitting by the roadside begging. [47] When he heard that it was Jesus of Nazareth, he began to shout, "Jesus, Son of David, have mercy on me!"

[48] Many rebuked him and told him to be quiet, but he shouted all the more, "Son of David, have mercy on me!"

[49] Jesus stopped and said, "Call him."

So they called to the blind man, "Cheer up! On your feet! He's calling you." [50] Throwing his cloak aside, he jumped to his feet and came to Jesus.

[51] "What do you want me to do for you?" Jesus asked him.

The blind man said, "Rabbi, I want to see."

[52] "Go," said Jesus, "your faith has healed you." Immediately he received his sight and followed Jesus along the road.

≥Little me≤
BIG GOD

Collect the series:

• The Man Who Would Not Be Quiet • Never Too Little
• The Best Thing To Do

For Ebyn.
Praying you'll believe in God's love and power, no matter what
others say, and find it to be true, as Bartimaeus did.
S. W.

The man who would not be quiet!
© Stephanie Williams, 2019

Published by:
The Good Book Company

thegoodbook.com | www.thegoodbook.co.uk
thegoodbook.com.au | thegoodbook.co.nz | thegoodbook.co.in

ISBN: 9781784983833 | Printed in India